The Children of None

Read the power of simple words!

STEVE ANC

COPYRIGHT

Copyright © 2020 by Steve Anc
The Children Of None

Published by Steve Anc
Website: www.ancpoems.com

For permission requests, write to the publisher at
Email: stvanc@gmail.com

Phone: (+234) 813-107-1433

All rights reserved. No part of this publication may be reproduced, distributed, or transmitted in any form or by any means, including photocopying, recording, or any other electronic or mechanical methods, without the prior written permission of the publisher, except in the case of brief quotations embodied in critical reviews and certain other noncommercial uses permitted by copyright law.

DEDICATION

To my late dad, Ajuzie Nwaorisara — behold your son!

To my mom, Ajuzie Nwaorisara Ihemamma.

To Katina Woodruff Borgersen for your amazing support and encouragement so far.

ACKNOWLEDGEMENT

I acknowledged everyone that has contributed their time to read my previous collection and also to YOU — you are amazing!

I will not fail to mention your name sir (Eleweke Kingsley), you have an amazing personality.

The Children Of None

The Children of None is a collection of 43 poems, each poem is written with a unique style and candor. Several poems within the collection stand out as inspirational, heartfelt, and rich in language. The author does an exceptional job of creating unique poems, on themes such as social justice, love of family, culture in Nigeria, and how the process of creating a poem. Each poem exhibits a fresh new perspective, enchanting rhyme, and language that beckons the reader to read the poems again and again.

Katina Woodruff Borgersen
CEO: One Stop Write Shop, LLC

This poem collection is absolutely a breath of fresh air! It speaks life into the souls of the hibernating. Mr. Steve Anc's style of poetry is definitely an awakening experience. The distinguished poet penned in his poem, *Children of None,* "Cause tomorrow is for the seers' astrologers said. Do not use the lens of now to measure our capabilities." This rings true for poet Steve Anc, as his wordsmanship will in time become airborne; the fresh air needed for many readers to come.

Kela Calvin
United States of America, Author

I have read most of the poems in this book and I'm a fan of them all. I must say that
"A poem to my momma" and "The power of simple words" were my favorite. The woman is the only being that can reproduce and I enjoyed reading how he appreciated his mother for that. Also sometimes we forget the significance of the simple things in life and including some small words because they can make a big difference. He did a great job at delivering 'the power of simple words.' Great poet!

Andrea Priest-Atkins, a poet.
United States of America

The Children Of None

Steve's work just gets better and better. This collection of fine work is packed full of some of his finest pieces including 'I am Alive', 'Chim Ama Nda' and 'Mask of Life'.

The set starts off strongly with 'What is Justice' and very rightly so, this piece sets the bar incredibly high leading the reader into a sense of emotional comfort from the soul.

Throughout the collection, Steve draws on Shakespearean influences and uses his talents as a writer to the best of his ability. In fact, I do believe this area of poetry is his strongest when not drawing inspiration from his own life and culture in all it's technicolour.

Steve shows he is one of the finest writers of poetry in the world right at this very moment and encourages us all to dive into the very pits of our stomachs whilst reading his work, knowing we are only more complete for doing so.

Tyler Heart, a poet.
United Kingdom

I enjoyed reading this collection of poems. The different topics held my attention well. Great book!

Sergeant Ronnie Atkins,
United States of America

"Do not use the lens of now to measure our capabilities - As the wind of morning blows wherever it wishes - We will stand in this porch to control our - Cause the wind will blow out of the dusty night - Not minding the Astrologer's prediction".

Amazing collection from Steve. Poems such as "The Power of Simple Words, We sipped Courage, Children of None and several others in this collection have shown how talented the Writer is in weaving words to create a nourishing effect for the mind.

Tobi Delly, Nigeria.
Author of The Ultimate Leverage, 25 things you must have before age 25 and "The Intelligent Self" book series.

Powerful poems with deep meaning that touches the heart and soul. Steve is a true poet and talented artist.

Jason Ng
Canada

For me it was an experience of sensing so many emotions all at once. I particularly loved the poem "Poem to my momma and your momma". The lines "My days I count as a naira note always wanting to make you proud" touched my heart. This was a little extra special because it made me think of my mother and how we children always want to make them proud. Also, extremely love the poem "My momma and my village river". After reading all the poems I felt these were things which are very close to your heart and you expressed them beautifully with your words. Bringing out the emotions you have un your heart into these poems. Thanks for sharing this with me.—

Smriti verma
India

Steve's poems reflect his deep dive into our social bond. It looks he has keenly studied different aspects of life and, he looks social genius. Although most of his poems are about love and affection, there are many where a social bond is discussed and while reading his poems it seems that the poet is a social scientist.

Muhammad Azad
Pakistan

TABLE OF CONTENTS

COPYRIGHT ... ii
DEDICATION ... iii
ACKNOWLEDGEMENT ... iv
PREFACE ... x
WHAT IS JUSTICE? ... 1
EVERYONE WILL GO ... 3
SMILE WITH ME ... 4
POEM TO MY MOMMA AND YOUR MOMMA ... 5
THE POWER OF SIMPLE WORDS ... 7
THE CHILDREN OF NONE ... 9
I AM ALIVE ... 11
CHIM AMA NDA ... 13
WHY I MARRIED MY WIFE ... 14
TO CALL OR NOT TO CALL ... 15
MY MOMMA AND MY VILLAGE RIVER ... 16
STILL WAITING FOR YOUR EMAIL ... 18
AM IN LOVE WITH A COMPLICATED GIRL ... 19
WE SIPPED COURAGE ... 21
MASK OF LIFE ... 22
HE SELECTED YOUR DAY ... 23
I WILL BE THERE ... 24
EPIGRAM OF GOOD WISHES ... 26
THE LAW OF CREATION ... 27
COUPLETS ON PRICELESS AND PERSONALITY ... 28

TILL THE OCEAN DRY 30

WHAT A FORMIDABLE THREAT 31

GOODBYE PLAYMATES... 32

BEHOLD YOUR SON 34

THE FIRST BATTLE OF PLANET EARTH 36

THE DYING LIGHT 39

MY JOY AND MY PYRAMID 41

COUNTING THE BEATS.. 42

SEEK HER 43

TORMENT OF THE DESTITUTE 44

WHAT IS AGWU?... 47

DESTINY UNFOLDS 49

DESCRPTION OF AMADI OHA 50

PAPA EXPLAINED THE UNKNOWN.............................. 51

ONYE KWE CHIN YA EKWE 53

THE WORLD LIVE IN PRETENSE.................................... 54

A REJECTED LOVER 55

BEST CHILDHOOD MEMORIES EVER 56

DON'T GOBBLE IT DOWN.. 58

BREAKING THE ENVIRONMENTAL CODE............................ 59

ENVISION A NARROW CHUTE... 60

ABOUT THE AUTHOR.. 62

The Children Of None

PREFACE

If you have read the first, second and the third poem in this book, don't say that you have started, you will say, 'I am about to start,' because the case opens the bracket... ' steve Anc

WHAT IS JUSTICE?

Where is justice?
The vibration on our feet is no longer for celebration,
Vengeance and agitation had taken the choristers voice'
The tune we used to dance with is dancing against us;
The talking drum had cloven apart by the thunderstorm,
The music we breathe out has been stolen.

Where is justice?
Whereas we fight with starvation than principalities,
We are at war with an enemy we can't win;
Oh, how can we win?
Aye! aye!

We are at war with our bellies as the bellyache,
The intestines are no longer friendly with the anus
They puff and puff to overthrow the tongue,
And the mouths aggressively yawn as dry saliva stoop to kill.

Where is justice?
We have been given to lawlessness and stateless society,
Freedom of thought buried under the symbol of justice;
Anarchy and tyrants had overthrown our king,
Alas, fighting the hands that feed a hearth home;
Dying for the peace they had fought for.

Where is justice?
Who haven't an ounce of oil task for a barrel of crude,
Who haven't a grain of corn task for a container of wheat;

The Children Of None

Able men dying with future peace and innovation,
Killing killed our killing king with no one to judge,
To hell with your filthy hands of equality, I said.

Where is justice?
Whereas sufficient had detached from our vocabularies,
It is not much fun dead being than been lead?
To cuddle up with the hands of our ancestors,
Kiss the dirty mouth of a graveyard
And dance with the corpse that stinks in the clay;
Of what benefits that tyrants reign?

I ask, "where is justice?"
Though father told me none queries the incubus,
To hell with the incubus, it can't put an iron on our brains;
Cause we can't think metallic,
And to the dead cheers come too late!

EVERYONE WILL GO

Proud thou not and think a dearest friend
Plot not the graph of arrogance
Nor study the Atlas of dishonesty
To avoid the dance of shame

Though nature had crafted thee with crystal
Coated thy person with abilities
Caved out uniqueness from nothingness
Please purchase a solemn heart
Grim thy time with fairest fame

No matter what it released to thee
For thy name to be plotted out
Tire the robe of simplicity
For the gift of everyone varies
By the kiss of luck one shines
By the thrust of fate another struggles

No matter how thou soweth and reapeth
Weigh thyself on the scale of humility
Let it be thy guide as thou navigate
Thrust not thy mates beneath the mat
Neither gives thy name to the beast of high horse

No matter how high thou aspire
Detach thy feet from haughty soil
Strife for a merciful lead
Plead for a humble end
Cause fabrics will wear out
Endless sleep is the end of all

SMILE WITH ME

Smile with me, my lily friend
I brought these lilies from the valley,
Cause I knew the thought of a needy heart;
Understood the breath of a thirsty soul,
Feel the gloomy look of the hungry eyes.

Though our skin varies in colors
Pigment painted some eyes blue, others green,
but the mouth can't deny the nose;
Neither shall the marble amount more than the man.

Despite the color competition in Grandma's teeth,
That departed with my appetite;
And the annoying voice of a psychopath,
I was not made of metals;
Nor had I detached the hands of empathy

Just the hands of luck that parted us,
But can't sleep the carpet on my feet;
Please let's paddle on the rocky leather chair,
My heart is beating bit a pat.

Smile with me, my lily friend,
Cause heart and hands worked in unison;
they had called your name from afar,
And the eyes blink in agreement
Cause I wore a compassionate heart.

POEM TO MY MOMMA AND YOUR MOMMA

You are the womb that bears the Earth
The Sac that loads the family
The hand that first held me close
The sound of my heartbeat
you first understood
Like the flip of a pancake
you wipe my tears

Long blonde hair, twirled in the wind
pretty enough to bring you some customers
Smile with eyes shining with gentle humor
Dark skin with pink lips
Innocence you find as you search her eyes
Very kind to strangers
as a glimpse into glory

My days, I count as naira note
always wanting to make you proud
Though the edge of my destiny is afire
Your heart is a prayer that pushes me up
I slice my prayer like an onion to thy
Maker,
asking Him to smoothen thy paths

I write you poem without heresies
You blanket my thoughts with caution
Kiss my forehead with words at my teen
Plant my feet on the path of hope
Your insanity then is my sanity now

Your affection is stronger than an

The Children Of None

affectionate kiss with closed eyes
As palpable as varicose veins
Glaring as diamond
Your tender kisses
 leave flowers in my memory

THE POWER OF SIMPLE WORDS

"Simple words move where big words stand!
They scan the wall of language,
As the captain scans the military zone
Head the wind's increasing scope.

Simple words understand the one-syllable word!
Spit out direction out of confusion,
Layout orderliness across a steep;
Act as antidotes to vocabularies,
Squeezed creative juices out of communication.

The wisdom of our ancestors' dwells in simple words!
Our elders communicate in simple words,
Cause comprehension comes without invitation;
As confusion leaves without notification.

They are rich with the right feelings!
Spice communication with the right taste
They give joy to the reader
And value to the writer,
Make poetry interesting to read.

They cut the edge of communication
injected charm in our eyes!
Dance, twist, turn mourning to singing
Brief and concise big words as a knife
that cut the edge of momma's garment.

They are like the spark in the night,
Lighting to the eyes of those who read!
They are the grace of prose
And the grease of poetry
It is difficult to enjoy the meal
of language without them!

The Children Of None

They are like a cobweb
Can catch big words,
Hold them up for all to see;
Some make you see,
The cold deep dark at night;
Others make you feel
The deepest pain in the heart,
Like rare stones in rings of gold
Or joy in the eyes of a child."

THE CHILDREN OF NONE

You may search our destinies with the conclusion of none,
  Owning nature did not send a smile on our days of
  conceptions;
    The rain of old money sat on the seat of contemplation:
    The pathways to excellently born were under
    construction,
      Favorable birth numbered us not worthy.

We may look common,
 On account of your conviction;
   Even the colored ones among us believe so,
    This thought was popular among the opulent,
      Sometimes we look uneasy as commoners in their
      presence.

 Through the lens of time, we had seen the glimpse of
 tomorrow,
   But a bit handicapped to do tomorrow
    Not that seats of qualifications were not available,
    Means of qualifications were not sent;
      Cause tomorrow is for the seers' astrologers said.

Do not use the lens of now to measure our capabilities,
  As the wind of morning blows wherever it wishes:
  We will stand in this porch to control our
   Cause the wind will blow out of the dusty night,
    Not minding the astrologers' prediction.

They fanned their premonstration and filled their

The Children Of None

expectation,
  Scattered their eyes like a tornado in search of our ends,
  Our names blow noisy sounds in their ears.
    But the voice that controls the wind shall loud our
    names,
      Saying, "we are not dying voices,
        But calculative eagles that hollo from the hill!"

I AM ALIVE

Though known as a rant and can't of a futile fork,
Selected from the community with breaking brittle;
And cast off as a cursed and a forsaken dice.
Ay, though they mock at me as a broken blade
Spat dusky spit at my feet,
Am alive!

Though darkly doom cloud me a glorious day,
Left me abaft in search of my personality;
Hoarse and drenched cheerfulness from my jaws,
Sent bitter odds as a mark of recognition;
Glorified the godforsaken hands of difficulties
And clothed me a person with the garment of a needy
Am alive!

Though the joy in me had sagged already,
And the memory of silver spoon in a swerve state,
Dangling as a yellow leave in a green plant;
Waiting to drop as a dying candlewick,
And buried in between the cloudy darky wall,
Am alive!

Though I was disqualified in a fearless fight,
And stripped off alight me earned right;
Filled me dignity with ornaments of shame.
They who triumph dotted me a person with a feeble mark,
As if they were setters of the trophy to heavenly race;
Am alive!

The Children Of None

Though the fig-tree didn't blossom as expected
Following through the horde of humanity
With dirty hands of Cameleon faeces on the wall
Back from the wall with a shattered heart in search
Am alive!

CHIM AMA NDA

Chim ama Nda
 So it rings
It rings to silent the noisy day
It rings to wake the silent night
It rings to spice the peaceful night
It rings to inject hope to the morning
It rings to paint happiness to our lips

Chi ama nda
So it vibrates
It vibrates from the angelic tongue
It vibrates as your parents agreed
It vibrates from my deepest being
It vibrates cause I believe in names

Chi ama nda
So it sings
It sings as a proclaimed song
It sings to brace up the home
It sings to brighten the frowning sky
It sings to support a falling feet
It sings to lift a drifting heart

Chim ama nda
In you, His loving light will shine
Your paths shall He bracing up
 Gives you wisdom as lightning

The Children Of None

WHY I MARRIED MY WIFE

"Oh, Lilian," I said,
"Correct my spellings when I err,
Though am a student of words
With a distinct accent—"
And she corrected me and said — "accent!"

"My dear," I said, "you are mine now,
Though you were your father's from inception;
You can look at my eyes and call me fiancé–"
And she smiled and said– "fiancé!"

"Oh my darling, you may memorize my account number,
But don't meditate on my account balance;
Cause the balance may be inconclusive–"
And she stammered and said– "inconclusive!"

"Dear Lilian," I said, "when I am dispirited
And Situation overwhelmed my reasoning,
Please support me with the pillar of hope–"
She nodded her head and said– "hope!"

"Correct my manner or my waggeries
When undue odds display in my actions,
Cause none is an island of knowledge;
But please spare my love for poetry–"
She looked at the window and whispered– "poetry!"

"The blood in my veins thirst for your presence,
And no more shall grammar and words cheat on us!
Therefore, will you be with me all the time–"
And she exclaimed and said– "all the time!"

TO CALL OR NOT TO CALL

Oh, Lilian! oh, darling Lilian, why did you?
My affectionate heart you have swayed,
Sued my fray self in your prison yard of fun;
Artfully, skinned off the self from centeredness.

Now I am more vulnerable to eleven digits,
As your thought shrinks my blood,
 to dial is my wish;
cause you had left your butterflies in my mind.

Sometimes, I wonder why can't I
To whisper me into enough is the call,
 Though, had left self on a frolic feather bed;
and became a man with a specific contact.
After all, we might get wed, my heart repeated,
Cause bloodline must flow, father instructed.

Oh Lilian! Oh dear Lilian! My Complex lilain!
Why did you wave to innocent nonchalant?
The 'call-free' me can't answer, but sits in regret,
Neither shall the 'mean' I withhold from you;
But to excuse me would have been the answer.
Alas, wish, you inform me not to go?
To cuddle you in my Elizabethan bond bed of roses.

Aye! My Lilian, this art of equality had lied to me,
I curse the day that told me that you shall call;
It has made a man into a woman.
Oh, Lilian! Darling Lilian!
Why did you make me think?
To call or not to call!

The Children Of None

MY MOMMA AND MY VILLAGE RIVER

I think that memory is the best
It leaves drops of ink in my mind
to read for rehearsal
Makes me borrow no forgetfulness
Strengthens my eyes-teeth
To bite the hands of time
And paint my lips with roses

It seats me in between thoughts
Gives me a sady-happy taste
Brings my village river to me
To ring and rinse my experiences
in Searches for momma's instructions
To rehearse what she had spat out
And laugh and twist my wit

I think her opinion is the best
Wisdom hangs between her lips
Her mouth had I kissed for a lead
Kissed the dusty of memory for remembrance

Though now grown and elegantly stand
Had gleaned in beaches and fiberglass pools
And more of words conscious
cause of rapid development
venture unto my garb of memory
cause still slightly a village boy
To dig out her instructions

The Children Of None

"In the village river, you shall wash
You shall not waste my water
Neither shall you waste my words
Let the reserved water be in the reservoir"
As she instructed, so shall I do
In egwu obilaji, shall I be

STILL WAITING FOR YOUR EMAIL

An early morning creature, once I was known,
I wake me at twilight to read what you left;
As a bird of twilit river.
Gobbled a cup and puffed my cheek,
Read numerous, but left a few to hang.

Sometimes left a dozen, cause of drowsy,
O'er the inbox, I left them to dangle;
As a deserted heart in a desert,
And cling my muscular teeth so tight
Cause enough had been seen, my mind sang.

A proud river was I given my mouth to—
To drink and wash away your importance,
To drink and thrust your name as a dusty mat,
To drink and forget your person that shades and shines,
To drink and see your emails as a burden.

Now I lay like an empty and a weightless cup,
Regretting my art of negligence in abeyance
In a lookout for the slightest notification,
To lick any ink, you had left;
Thinking the beep was your mail.

I wake like a weary and worried wife every day,
Waiting for the moon from the blizzard border;
To bring the previous ink of your pen
To make the best of it.

My mind craves for you in sorto moment
Ready to burry self-centeredness and drowsiness
Value, will I tag on you and keep a light heart
Hang the flag of human importance.

AM IN LOVE WITH A COMPLICATED GIRL

What put me in a rage
Is the look on your face
As it glee and spleen
Ceases the singers of the sky
Slaughters their orchestration
Makes the angels gasp
Inject complications

When love chose you
I wore a kind hat
Cause love is kind
Is evil of the mind
Not to be kind
But the more I heart you
The more you harden your heart

When I slaughtered laughter
You executed a frown face
Then I sent for pillar of war
Your feedback was peace
Neither heaven nor earth
Men of valor nor feeble men
Can straighten your personality

I, that love spaces of stars
And harmony of the universe
With the tranquility of the sea
Now convict in darkest wall
And endure earthly hell

Please pray me no psalmist
Nor preach me any Chronicles

The Children Of None

No need to preach nor pray
Just teach my heart to hate
I had purchased complications
From your market

The Children Of None

WE SIPPED COURAGE

You deem it far from pleasant
That majority starve with emptiness,
To deprive sustenance, you projected as a dart;
And perchance makes thousands hurt,
As it added fat to your heart.

Coward remains cowards, till sipped guts,
We had masqueraded as chicken, cause of division;
Our rights, you got associated with,
Dwarfed our courage and hang embargo on our sleeves.

Many a man is tasty, cause he fears your footprint,
So, before the shore, he faltered!
He dares not approach, causes woe to individual courage;
Though he plays the flutes of a piper at home.

Many among the cowards had eaten the heart of a lion,
As ready as the clock in search of your soul;
Gave up their sweet-savory, chew the bitter leave of revenge,
With blaring stomach and heroic eyes.

We were well fed up to the
mouth when life beginnings,
Till principality as you, insist;
Took the meals of millions,
To keep afloat your big name.

MASK OF LIFE

So oft' in the mid of night
   I wake me in my bed
With utter panic plastered on my chest
   The door was flailing like a storm
The roof that should have kept me warm flew away

The floor sagged but silent as a graveyard
   And feet cemented as agama lizard
Mind wandered beyond my confined walls
   In quest of why folks masked

The folks at home, masked,
   The folks in the street, also masked
Therefore, walk and walk to mask me
   To mask the breath from my nostril
And to mask the words as they escape
   Just to scrap my name from the book of disobedience
   Cause I neither cough nor sneeze

Have them masked as normalcy?
   Whence comes to this gloomy veil
In the darkest night, I lie
   Thinking in agony and snoopy for remedy
   And soliciting to God as a question
Is this mask for life"

HE SELECTED YOUR DAY

Though I lie with the scrum of thoughts
Your birthday outdoes all thoughts
Gazing to gold seraph wing at my porch
With wistful wonder in my eyes
And a sincere look in search of a date
In the midst of months for an accurate month

Upon the paradise of creation
Upon the day of delivery
Oh there she is
A precious daughter
That glitters in midst of gloom

How ardently will I aspire
To see you soar celestially high
And mingle with your divine callings
And swift on crystal wings

As the poet selects his words
So did your Marker select your world
With a purpose for all to see
And a mission for you to accomplish

I WILL BE THERE...

Wherever there is peace
I will be there...
Wherever there is a need to correct corrections
I will be there...
A fight for united understanding
I will be there...
Wherever there is a humanist
I will be there...
Teaching for peace of the universe
I will be there...

Wherever there is a child
I will be there...
A child praying to God in heaven
I will be there...
To memorize how he express' himself
I will be there...
To greet him with thunderous amen
I will be there to laugh with him for answered prayers
And to bring down the floor of heaven

Wherever folks hang around
I will be there...
Wherever they celebrate their achievements
I will be there...
Wherever neighbors raise their voices
I will be there...
Neither to add fuel to the flame
Nor to praise their waves of anger
I will be there...
To hold their fists not to hit

The Children Of None

Wherever there is truth
I will be there...
Or, I think there is a man of integrity
I will be there...
Wherever I see hope spring out from human breast
I will be there...
Cause hope marketh no ashamed
Wherever, passion leads
I will be there...
As passion works his works

Wherever lives wisdom, beauty, and increase
I will be there...
To separate wisdom from witty
I will be there...
To see the vice, translate into virtue
I will be there...
Cause war and death are examples of epistrophe

EPIGRAM OF GOOD WISHES

Am sorry I can't type again
My fingers are crying
My heart is in the house
I must pause till it comes
 back to me
To prepare for this great feast
Oh behold
Here it comes
 It comes with gift
And glittering hands of good wishes
With tongue ready to declare
That all the world shall see
I have known seconds and minutes
Have known weeks and months
But haven't seen the 4th of April
Without you to celebrate
I have seen roses damasked
I have seen the Earth covered with cloud
But no such roses shall come to your paths
Neither shall thy paths gloomy
Cause I love to see you shine
Also in abundance, you will appear daily
Nothing of you shall fade away
Neither shall you suffer a misfortune

The Children Of None

THE LAW OF CREATION

How jocund the human race will have been
If everyone will understand the law 'f creation:
As Manatees and guppies dwell
without enormity but conformity;
In a dewy and breeze precinct,
Instead of a fiery and flaming whack.

Do not think I write to joke!
Neither joke with my write!
Caus' pure reason 's i' the armpit of well-meaner.
 Inoculat'd that all creatures need life,
Also shouldn't parry from the shelter;
Thus imagine how it thrusts in thirsty
for water.

How lovely compassionate parents passionately,
 Stoop to the ground and kiss their lily ones;
Truly I just wear such a mind for little creatures.

In sublime and with the simplicity of thought I solicit,
Enow the hatred of the poor brute:
Men should school in unity with fauna.

How healthy is the breezeway as 't   sniffs to sip,
And how it wings with saucy flossy
Below the basement of the tardy path
Sipping for living.

So let m' sing the lyrics of the Wirick's without satiric,
Asking how blithe the world will lithe
If everyone had fore-saw the law of creation?

COUPLETS ON PRICELESS AND PERSONALITY

I

In the great walk of life, we will all walk alone
And only the unbroken state can bear our feet on the way to the throne.

II

Rectitude is priceless but such warm fools vilify
Who relished today with a fragment of tomorrow.

III

Here is someone who grows weaker in insidious and treacherous
And stronger in sincerity what he lost in wily.

IV

Integrity is zealous for the mutual interest of humanity
While fools possessed places for their zeal.

V

Integrity gain strength by profound exactness
As one betwixt prowess, benison and blithe.

VI

Wouldn't I write for the palates of this priceless douceur
Purge all my verses and stanzas from the sign of insanity.

VII

For the pen reveals the author's creed
They praise no works than fallacy and delusion
I applaud the priceless gift of integrity in a personality.

The Children Of None

TILL THE OCEAN DRY

"Do not approach the strand with two legs,
Cling caution on your shoulder as conspicuous birds;
Don't be befooled by the opinion of the bathers," Papa said.

Obedient to your words, had I adhered as an oath,
But disobedient is the best remedy as I approach;
Better the unborn to confer with death than to declare adieu to the carrier.

Lo, uphold your son papa!
Is already raging as a phage,
Behold the oceanic tempest from Atlantic;

But my feet had I knot underneath the sea as duck,
Never to be moved by the oceanic current;
I can see the nautical sway from the West–

Rushing as fast as the brown bear,
Calling it host to sift me like a weightless shaft;
Querying my constancy in the midst of the tempestuous.

Feet will I move not, cause stability was I found upon,
Here will I commune, not minding the conquest;
Here will I stand, till the ocean dry!

WHAT A FORMIDABLE THREAT

Never had I dreamt it would be so anon,
In reality, I now stood to avouch;
On a dreary stage was I drenched
Asking: why shall it be in this- domain?

Should I lament in my closet-
Or bewail loudly and chide the silly conceit?
Time will bring relief; the elders had taught!
But where is the time to ease me from this fraught?

Let the dusty wind from the east gale and wipe this sorrow away,
Rather be castrated of this memory than left alone to wallow.
Let impromptu rainfall to shed my tears abroad,
Rather than the droplets of tears to dry on my abode.

The pain bites so deeper than metaphoric phrases,
But the elders painted the phrases though they had no teeth!
I want him back at these dark shrinking knees,
So tell me no tale that softens the head but hollows the heart.

Paint my face with rapture,
Let me know that the end is at hand;
For the joy of living had been stolen by the ashes of loneliness,
Death poses as formidable force!

The Children Of None

GOODBYE PLAYMATES

Oh, years! And my playmates! Adieu:
Ave the ten years Chinomso Iroha-
My childhood comrade.
Goodbye, the pears on the roadside.
Valedictory the wheeling vehicle-
My only means of transportation.
Behold I now dwell in adulthood
Where I do nothing than to scheme:
Scheming for beaucoup ways of how
Deeming for a better tomorrow.
My eyes have seen since we parted
Nonage images still abide in me.
Sometimes I am lost in the Sea-
Thinking how time flies to nirvana.
In my lonely solarium, I sit daily,
Always asking rhetorical questions:
Does the moon still sway at night?
Are there still stars in the sky at night?
Were they deluged by the endless day?
Everything seems too abridge now
cause I measure with achievement,
Not with the formal insouciant lad.
 In grief, I abide in sometimes,
Cause I now imagine the impossible.

The Children Of None

But still not as free as I used to be
Please give me an hour to play again,
That was my gentle disposition then.
Cause football, I am not good at.
In Wrestling, consider me not worthy.
But here as an adult, I stand today,
Asking for permission to declare
Total freedom from insouciant lad-
Heaving up my hands to heavens
Lifting them to say,
Bon, voyage playmates!

BEHOLD YOUR SON

I was not aware that I could
I would have told you to bide
But man does not know tomorrow
I would have predicted that then

What a predicament to be in
That man cannot see his future
I would have told you horrendous tale
How the dark unlighted gave way
And the bubblehead became bright

I thought you could have waited
I would have chant how it all began
How fate gifted me with words
As her lips kissed my forehead

I thought you would have waited
I would have shown you the abrupt
How I was graced by God that knows
When the passing bell doth-rang

I wish you would have waited
I would have chronicled how it started
How the tappers burn blue
When the comforters are few

The Children Of None

But who am I to quest for the quietus
Cause no one queries the incubus
I am just Steve Anc (Chimezie)
Yet in despond and pain, I sat
With the quest to still query

I was not aware that I could
 When I lie in my bed as a lad
Sick in head and weak at heart
 And with doubt of self-esteem
I would have told you to wait

Dedicated to late Mr. Ajuzie Nwaorisara

THE FIRST BATTLE OF PLANET EARTH

The world is chaotic!
The world is confused,
As the drunken bee.
As confused as the restaurant's look!

Human minds had set ajar!
A strong west wind is here to devour,
Like the grinding under the skin;
No news connotes joyousness.
The Arab has lost in camel race!
The whole world is in aberration
We still safari in wonder,
The planet Earth is in the erratic.

The bar of soap is no longer a beautiful cake!
Just a shamble of news slaughtered the earth!
The world is at war with a hidden enemy!
The weather stings like an angry bee in search of prey,
Not as pure as drifted snow as it used to;
The silent night has become an ace of danger!

As the ragged continents row by
So did humanity watch rolling
This is a moment of silence;
There are many sorrows in the air
The world has shutdown already,
Everyone looking for ideas!
People don't know what to think again
Even I cannot help thinking,
Cause thinking is made ritualistic;
Confusion had set in already.

The Children Of None

Predictors and astrologers are in moody state:
Intimacy had proved abortive,
Intimate contact withheld totally
Tissue paper is in the highest demand,
Face mask and hand glove as a panacea
Countries had shutdown
Social distance at an alarming rate,
Goods are vanishing within a blink;
And no remedy for regulation yet!

Who is shooting at us from behind?
Who is behind this pandemic outbreak?
Who has done this to humanity?
Who mixed our breathing with the air of panic?
May vengeance grip thee by the hair,
And beat bad intention out of your skin!

Our inner strengths are been sapped,
Can this be the end of humanity?
People asking many why's:
Why why why and why it echoed along,
People took a recession as a remedy;
Is better than connecting to humanity
Cause the connection will lead to contamination.

I have not heard secession commonly said before,
But is like the anthem now.
People are living in isolated Ireland
The Bell is ringing for remedy,
Many are quarantined already;
Some suffering in respiratory difficulty
Why the death rate at an alarming rate.

The Children Of None

When will this yellow river clear?
The heart of compassion had locked down.
I have not learned to be certain about anything,
Until the thing becomes certain
And certainty becoming certain
This is a certain situation

We will overcome this pandemic
We can soften the harsh realities,
Despite the falling ashes;
To soak in the baths of padigi beach
Cheering until the box crack.

The Children Of None

THE DYING LIGHT

The dream and purpose that I saw
Had tricked down my face like tears
I wandered lonely as a cloud
Floating on high over hollows and hills
And all the best of the dark I have met
All the best of light I have forsaken
From the first fourteen days to fourteen night
Have seen death!

The lights, and the paths that I saw
Now lay afloat as a stark
As my heart losing out its true nature
Like one that has been seven days drowned
In seven days and seven nights' lockdown

The life that I saw
Now made way for death
Though I wish not to wait for death
Cause I could not even wait for death after all
Death will surely wait for me
 Let me first speak dagger to its heart as it waits

Seven days, seven nights, I saw a cause
 Why hungry eyes bawl
A cause why hungry legs totter
A cause why hungry hands tremble.

As stomach drags me to the end of the Street
So did my feet drag back to the end of the house
With garment of shame as a veil
 Stomach stirring as stirring tea
And worms roaring as roaring lions

The Children Of None

Let me but dust my bed, waiting for a dusty night
Allowing the last ink to ooze from the pen
Better to be numbered with the mark of death
For too late I would have rung the bell for injustice
Neither shall I be chain on the path of starvation any longer

Hope had leaked out from my soul
Death had seeped through the sole of my soul
Cause in the vile and ingrate nation I dwell
Let me pour away the ocean and rinse the shore
Too late shall it repent!

MY JOY AND MY PYRAMID

Only a little more
I have to write:
Not to dwell in my thoughts,
But to give thanks to God
For peaceful and love home;
And the grace to abide together.

Life is but a flying minute!
Better to fly in merriment
Or safari in harmony,
Than dwell in hostility;
Cause divided will fall.

Life is pleasant with
good memories;
Though time runs
without notification,
With scare leaves of memories
Scattered on the roof of oneness
Ready to be lifted by air of
Wonderful gathering.

How many days have I forgotten?
But never will I forget this day
Cause celebration day it is,
Though wasn't around;
But happy to see hearts rejoiced.
That is my joy
And my pyramids.

The Children Of None

COUNTING THE BEATS

Counting the beats
Counting the slowness of babies steps,
Counting the sophistication of babies dance,
Counting the ennui look from nauseate hearts;
The bleeding end of anticipation,
Hasten winky eyes of time
And the eagerness of wakeful mind.

Counting the turbulent days without sun,
Counting the long nights without a moon,
The dusty Sahara harmattan wind;
The colossal turning of morning noisome.
And the great anticipation to mask the head underneath
From a bitter sky!

O, may I ask
How long shall we bear the whips and scorns of time?
Whereas, pain strikes without deliberation!
O where then shall we be–
Whenever we are whelmed of trying?
Not there is no known place as "there"
But was only reserved for the courageous!

Countless times had we tried,
Also, countless times had we beaten by the trials;
But only if we can overlook the falling ashes,
Once more shall only we try:
Who cares if failure knock us off a thousand times,
Cause humans minds are more elastic
Forgetting our mistakes and lapses within a blink.

SEEK HER

Seek and Yee shall find!
Men live on without recognizing
 her presence.

Here comes a moment in history when nothing quantifies.
When wealth and connections desert men in the city of oblivion.
A moment when humanities judge base on the content of character not on charisma.

Forgive us, you might say, for we know not what we do.
But here comes a moment in history when ignorance is no longer a forgivable offense.
A moment when only she has the power to resolve it.

With purity of conscience, she bequeathed to you all the gift of hope and salvation of tomorrow.
And yet there are men who hate her like a plague, fueled by self-righteous that they can do without her.

There is the silver-haired being who carelessly calls her imperfect.
she is not a prophet.
She is your guide.

TORMENT OF THE DESTITUTE

Oh, nature!
Dispel from this darkness in their paths
Clothe their minds with the garment of pure reasoning
Save them from their blind folly
Life has grown uneven,
though they are thy handmade.

Oh, nature!
Things seemly grow unseemly
The friendly plans have become a thorn to their thoughts
Neither hear nor behold in their state,
the law that divinity brings;
which the privileged obeyed.

Oh, nature!
They are aimlessly straying in the paths of ignorable strife
Men with zeal unblest,
 that are wearied to become
Men with a baser quest,
that are turned to mockery and shame.

Oh, nature!
Deliver they that are shrouded in ignorance
and bathed in the riverside of destitute
That them, being honored may
 honor and respect thy name
No worrier trusted in thee.

The Children Of None

Oh, nature!
Though great first cause,
Least understand
Whose all my sense and thought to originate from,
remember the destitute

SHOT STORIES

The Children Of None

WHAT IS AGWU?

It was a blissful afternoon, and I was on a bus around the third mainland bridge Lagos, Nigeria. I was reading one of my favorite books (Outwitting the Devil by Napoleon Hill), then I was interrupted by a question from a man abbreviated as MM and fully named Mad Madico.

He asked with his British accent, "What is Agwu?"

I responded, "when I was younger without experience I imagine that the story of the land is easy, that anyone of us can get up and tell it. But that is not so. Not so about AGWU!

Agwu does not call a meeting to choose his seers and diviners or artists.
Agwu, the god of healers;
Agwu the brother of Madness!

Born in the same womb with Madness, but he and madness were not created by the same chi__.

Agwu is the right hand a man extends to his fellows; Madness, the forbidden hand.

Madness unleashed and rides his man roughly into the wild Nzeogwu market. Whereby Agwu, possesses his own just as securely but have him corralled to serve the compound.

Agwu picks his disciple, ring his eyes with white chalk and dips his tongue, willing or unwilling, in the brew of prophecy; immediately, the man will speak and put head and tailback to the severed trunk of our tale. He is the liar who can sit under his thatch and see the moon hanging in the sky outside.

The Children Of None

This miracle man with the chalked eye will see every blow in a battle he never fought. Especially, when he looked around him and found no age-mate to challenge his claim--he will turn the mark inflicted to him by chicken-pox and said he suffered in childhood into bullet scars.

The lies of those possessed by Agwu are lies that do not harm anyone. They float on top of the story like bubbling at the top-mouth of new palm-wine.

DESTINY UNFOLDS

His picture buoyed around my wall as wind wanting to escape from wind van or should I say wind of destiny.

"But I have begotten thee, my son... Be still and know that I am God...." Whispered to me by a Voice, as an audible as a gift, to relay to you.

I know presently, you are confronted by the sea of uncertainty, sitting in the wall of childhood playfulness. But one day, a multitude of people will witness this childish display of yours.

I so much believe in you, because I have no friends called Thomas to scruple my inclination, nor brother named Nathaniel to vilify your environment, neither do I have a wife called Jezebel that can influence my prowess and sagacity.

But boy remember this: my profession enjoins me to maintain discretion. I mean absolute discretion on a point like this!

But I chose to break the protocol. Yes, I want to go against natural phenomenal to reply you.

"Your greatest risk is your childhood friends, those who grow up with you in your village. Keep them at arm's length, you will leave long."

DESCRPTION OF AMADI OHA

He never seemed to be bothered about anything. He had no wife called Nwanyibuego to be scared of, nor son call Chukwumma to care for, neither daughter called Ugodiya to instruct.

He had no compound of his own. His small house was in his younger brother's compound.

Yes was getting too old for active farming, so his yams were few, and he owned very little property. He was friendly to everyone and was highly respected.

His office like the high priest of the most powerful gods lent him great dignity.

PAPA EXPLAINED THE UNKNOWN

...his laughter vanished as it had come---that is, without warning or leaving footprints--as a sign to remember what triggered the laughter.

It was a kind of laughter one sometimes heard from a masked ancestral spirit. He would salute you by name and asked if you knew who he was.

Then he might laugh again as if through a throat of metal. And the meaning of the laughter was that son, you might not understand the meaning of what thou seeketh.

You are the only person in this Abia State, I mean Nigeria or should I say the whole Africa or whole wide world that did not know the meaning of Osu.

I laughed at my ignorance but he frowned at it because he expected me to know many things.

Then I asked him, "Papa what exactly is Osu? Please explain so that those that read my write-up will know."

He responded, 'Osu is like leprosy in the mind of our people. An outcast. Dedicated to the gods of our land. A sacred family!

The Children Of None

Please my son, don't bring Osu lady into my family. If you do, your children and your children's children unto the third generation will curse your memory. It is not for my sake I speak my son, my days are few. You will bring sorrow to your head and the head of your children.

Think of that, my son. Who will marry your daughters? Whose daughters will your sons marry?'

The Children Of None

ONYE KWE CHIN YA EKWE

As I leaned on the pedestrian bridge and cast my mind on the wheel of life; ruminating on better ways to live it, the saying of the elders, "onye kwe Chi ya ekwe!", was relayed from within.

I was stunned by this strange realization, though I was fully conscious, there was no more inflow of thoughts to discard the previous axiom. Then I felt drawn into what seemed like a vortex of energy and uncontrollable eruption.

At first, it was a slow movement; as slow as leaking sachet of water, then it accelerated. I was gripped by intense fear and my hands started to tremble. I heard the word, "you are not good enough!" as if an arrow shot at me from behind. I could feel sucked into a void immediately.

But suddenly, I felt unspeakable sensation.
There was no more fear.
I was lifted my unknown force from the void.
Self-confidence and high self-esteem flushed out the pain by the previous arrow.

Without any more thought, I felt, I knew, there is more to what we can see with our necked eyes.
We are better than what the voice said.
We are the best version of ourselves.
There will never be another us in this world or the one come.
Thanks
I got up and said to myself with strong affirmation again, "onye kwe Chi ya ekwe!"

THE WORLD LIVE IN PRETENSE

That is it!
You can use this as a bargaining point.
The world lives on pretense.
Help it along.

Job title also can be used as euphemisms for the inevitable menial or unpalatable work that must be done.

A sewer worker becomes a "SANITATION ENGINEER, shoe cobbler, becomes
"GUCCI CEO"

This softens the pain of the sweat and slurs that go with such jobs.

Some Mob watchers claim that the title "BOSS OF ALL BOSSES" was eliminated because it created jealousy and animosity among the heads of the organizations.

All the bosses wanted to be equal, none wanted to be subordinated.

Even the creation of a national electoral commission is with a one-man, one-vote policy.

A REJECTED LOVER

There were myriad of thoughts on Ifesinachi's mind as he sat on the lonely path. He wore his sadness around his neck like a necklace made of stone.

His feelings were so mixed that it took him a long period to sort them out. "Why must she respond in such a manner?" he questioned himself as he sat in silence.

Ugodiya's NO to him at that moment was as fresh as words selected from today's newspaper; but because of love covereth all things, he acted as though it lacked bitterness at the moment.

"This was my first real encounter with a matured and beautiful lady and I had failed. Was I not reasonably good looking? I was not unduly shy; I could talk to girls fairly easily. Why then did I behave like a carved wooden figure before her?" These questions thrust itself into Ifesunachi's mind.

... Ifesinachi had studied her for a moment. It appeared her mind was far away from the conversation ground. But there was no knowing since she looked down and her long eyelashes completely obscured what the lids failed to cover. He made up his mind to cross over to her. As he drew in one leg preparatory to rising, Ugodiya raised her head and looked at him in the face and said NO...

He winced, then tried to smile but fail. His attempt to say another thing ended in a stammer. Clumsily he stretched out his hands to hold her but in his confusion, he misjudged the distance and his hands fail to reach her...

BEST CHILDHOOD MEMORIES EVER

My momma said, "Do not take it at heart chii, after all, you have fallen him in wrestling match last eke day. Your personal Chi was not at home that was how I view it."

Also, our people have a saying, "a man's god may be away on a journey on the day of an important fight and that may make all the difference."

...immediately I guessed igbozuruike's intention. Though we had quarreled a few days back at a small riverbank.

I am slightly-build a well-proportioned average young man, but Igbozuruike had a narrow square head(ax-head according to villagers) and an iroko trunk. Worst still he had a temper as bad as of a man with lows on his ten fingers.

"...we have had enough of the word, let's use our hands too. If you think that we are age-mate cross this line...

I leaped for a flying tackle. Igbozuruike sank on one knee, collected me on his shoulder, and flung me heavily on the ground. I disengaged myself and waited for him to use one of my deadly tactics.

For several minutes we pushed one another, treading down bushes like antelopes caught in a rope trap.

At last, I got under his armpits and began to push him back at full speed hoping that some undergrowth grass would entangle his two legs and make him fall. It almost happened, but as Igbozuruike was about to fall, he turned slightly sideways, engaged me on the floor with numbers of blows.

DON'T GOBBLE IT DOWN

Money answereth all things" the Bible declared. And our people said, "when a rich man is sick a beggar goes to visit him and say sorry. When the beggar is sick, he waits to recover and then goes to tell the rich man that he had been sick."

It is on this emblem that a man who has achieved great wealth in lands and livestock now wishes to pin an eagle's feather on his success by buying admission into the powerful and highest hierarchy of -ozo for total recognition.

But here comes he who understood the saying of the Bible and elders but lives inversely proportional.
A leader without a title.
A monk that sold his Ferrari.
A gobbler!

Life without savings and investments into the future is more difficult and more complex than the succession of hot and cold flushes of malaria.

While gobbling all down your stomach, remember your generations.

Old age is ticking faster than we can imagine.
Don't gobble it down!

BREAKING THE ENVIRONMENTAL CODE

I come from a place known as the clash of Titans figuratively.

A land where destinies were birth amid thorns and future seems bleak and pale.

I come from a place where humans work hand in hand with universal law to replace a vibrant and docile mind with indocility and complacency.

A place where difficulties will gaze at you directly and say, "guy do your worst." And challenges always eager to envelop your sense of focus.

I come from a land where creative minds give in to frivolity and vibrant youths to façade ideologies and unproductive idiosyncrasies.

So I grew up to read stories of men who have failed, but here comes a fearless being. A being who directly or indirectly had trained his mind and body to see beyond the present for the joy ahead.

A being who has sincerely learned to trust the void of the land and use it as stairways to his journey to the limitless sky.

A being who had seen the glory ahead and endured the pain and frustration.

You are the being!

ENVISION A NARROW CHUTE

There were shadows all around, the environment seemed unfamiliar and threatening as he sat.
His breath puffed dust in the stillness.
His eyes scanned the darkest corner of the vicinity in search of light.

The panting from his breath was a clear definition of uncertainty and fear.
But the look in his eyes revealed his deepest thought of readiness.

Of course, there had been times when we had been curious to know what the future hold.
To know what lay beyond the hedge people have predicted for us.
To know how and when the parental promises will begin to yield results.

To know when the universe and mother nature would recognize our resilience and sagacity and declare "congratulations."

Remember: gravitational law is against you already.
Thoughts midst with a feeling of complacency, the eyes clouded with the web of impossibilities.

The Children Of None

But keep the hope alive,
don't give up
and don't give in yet to challenges.
Look beyond the environment,
envision yourself in a narrow chute, where nothing pushes
you than the glory ahead.

ABOUT THE AUTHOR

Though Steve Anc had written hundreds of poems, he doesn't claim to be a poet; but a lover of words and so passionate for poetry. He loves words for its own sake, but it doesn't make him a poet, because poets are uniquely born.

Steve Anc's style of poetry is an awakening experience, and he shows that he is one of the finest writers on poetry in this world at this period we live.

Steve Anc is a student of psychology and graduate of political science with a popular slogan, "I am a lover of words!"

Book Review By Katina Woodruff Borgersen
CEO: One Stop Write Shop, LLC

The Children of None is a collection of 43 poems, each poem is written with a unique style and candor. Several poems within the collection stand out as inspirational, heartfelt, and rich in language. The author does an exceptional job of creating unique poems, on themes such as social justice, love of family, culture in Nigeria, and how the process of creating a poem. Each poem exhibits a fresh new perspective, enchanting rhyme, and language that beckons the reader to read the poems again and again.

The Power of Simple Words
The first time I read the poem, The Power of Simple Words, a smile came over me and I had to return to the poem to read it multiple times. What is most unique about this particular poem is how the author weaves in elements of writing such as using simple words to express thoughts on important subject matters.

> The wisdom of our ancestors' dwells in simple words!
> Our elders communicate in simple words,
> Cause comprehension comes without invitation;
> As confusion leaves without notification.

Words, whether long or short can affect communication in families and when writing poetry. A poem can be written using a direct style, that focuses primarily on the theme and not only the words were chosen.

The Children Of None

The two lines that stood out in the poem are in the last stanza:

They are the grace of prose
And the grease of poetry

What the author has conveyed in these two lines is: the words chosen for the poem or prose can be anything that is desired by the author and it makes little difference if the words are eleven syllables long, or as short as one-syllable words. His focus for the poem is on the words that make up poetry, prose, and other forms of literature. It's a fresh perspective on how a poet, uses and creates new and unique poems.

The Children of None
When I read the poem, The Children of None, I was amazed at the craftsmanship of the poems and how the author showed the issues that are often faced for people living in Nigeria.
The first stanza in the poem stood out the most and has become my favorite stanza within the entire collection.

> You may search our destinies with the conclusion of none,
> Owning nature did not send a smile on our days of conceptions; The rain of old money sat on the seat of contemplation:
> The pathways to excellently born were under construction,
> Favorable birth numbered us not worthy.

The rest of the poem is about the changing time, the change in culture and the change in a rapidly growing community – people, all seeking something similar, a chance to grow, to become educated, to create new opportunities, all with the attitude that life is possible, for all!

The Children Of None

Additional Favorite Lines:
Through the lens of time, we had seen the glimpse of tomorrow,
But a bit handicapped to do tomorrow
What an extraordinary poem, full of life and hope.

The third poem that I found most alluring was:
In the first battle of planet Earth, in this well-crafted poem, the poet describes the world as being, "Chaotic, Confused and Erratic," which resonates with the struggles many countries in the world face today. The author talks about the Covid-19 Virus, the shutdown, and pain that the world faces in terms of climate change, economy, and fear, which has increased within several months.

The bar of soap is no longer a beautiful cake!
Just a shamble of news slaughtered the earth!
The world is at war with a hidden enemy!
The weather stings like an angry bee in search of prey,
Not as pure as drifted snow as it used to;
The silent night has become an ace of danger!

One of my favorite stanzas in the collection:

Tissue paper is in the highest demand,
Face mask and hand glove as a panacea
Countries had shutdown
The social distance at an alarming rate,
Goods are vanishing within a blink;
And no remedy for regulation yet!

The Children Of None

While taking this new and exciting journey, reading and reviewing the collection, The Children of None, I realized something important about the author's writing style, he exuberates a serious yet informative style into many of his poems. The language and word choices are simple, poignant, and often, breathtaking.

I truly enjoyed my time reading and evaluating both of his poetry collections and I encourage everyone to buy a copy of the book and share these poems with their friends and family members. You will enjoy the collection as much as I have.

Made in the USA
Monee, IL
11 April 2021